WOMEN OF THE BIBLE

Activity Book

Women of the Bible Activity Book

Bible Pathway Adventures® is a trademark of BPA Publishing Ltd.
Defenders of the Faith® is a trademark of BPA Publishing Ltd.

ISBN: 978-1-989961-73-5

Author: Pip Reid
Creative Director: Curtis Reid

For free Bible resources including coloring pages, worksheets, puzzles and more, visit our website at:

www.biblepathwayadventures.com

◦◇ INTRODUCTION ◇◦

Enjoy teaching your children about the Bible with our *Women of the Bible Activity Book*. Packed with fun Bible quizzes, worksheets, coloring pages, and puzzles to help educators just like you teach children about the Biblical faith. Includes ESV scripture references for easy Bible verse look-up, and a handy answer key for educators.

Bible Pathway Adventures helps educators teach children the Biblical faith in a fun creative way. We do this via our illustrated storybooks, Activity Books, and printable activities –available on our website: www.biblepathwayadventures.com

Thanks for buying this Activity Book and supporting our ministry. Every book purchased helps us continue our work providing free Classroom Packs and discipleship resources to families and missions around the world.

The search for Truth is more fun than Tradition!

◇ TABLE OF CONTENTS ◇

EVE

Read Genesis 2:1-4:26.
Answer the questions below.

1. From which part of Adam's body did God make Eve?   ....

2. In which garden did God place Adam and Eve?   ....

3. Why did Adam name his wife Eve?   ....

4. Which creature tricked Eve into eating forbidden fruit?   ....

5. From which tree in the garden did Eve eat?   ....

6. How did God curse Eve for disobeying Him?   ....

7. What reason did Eve give God for eating the fruit?   ....

8. When Adam and Eve saw they were naked, what did they do?   ....

9. Where did God send them after they ate from the tree of knowledge?   ....

10. What were the names of Adam and Eve's five children?   ....

Eve was the first woman.
Unscramble the words to learn about the people
and places mentioned in this story.

aAdm	....	blAe	....	
neEd	....	mnowa	....	
eEv	....	nma	....	
petrnse	....	anCi	....	

✳ Read the story of Adam & Eve in Genesis 1:26-4:7 (ESV).

Let's Review

1. The serpent deceived Eve by...
2. What could Eve's life teach me?
3. Summarize her story
in 4-6 sentences.

....

....

....

....

....

....

....

....

....

....

....

....

....

SARAH

Read Genesis 12:1-23:20.
Answer the questions below.

1. Where were Abraham and Sarah born?

....

2. To which land did God tell Abraham and Sarah to go?

....

3. What was Sarah's original name?

....

4. Why did Sarah and Abraham go to the land of Egypt?

....

5. Why did God send great plagues on Pharaoh?

....

6. How old was Sarah when she had a baby?

....

7. What name did Abraham and Sarah give their son?

....

8. Who did Sarah demand leave the camp after Isaac was born?

....

9. What did Sarah and Abraham's son carry for his sacrifice?

....

10. Where did Abraham bury Sarah when she died?

....

Sarah & Abraham's journey

Read Genesis 12. Sarai and Abraham left the city of Ur and traveled to the land of Canaan.

Trace Sarai and Abraham's journey on the map by connecting the dots.

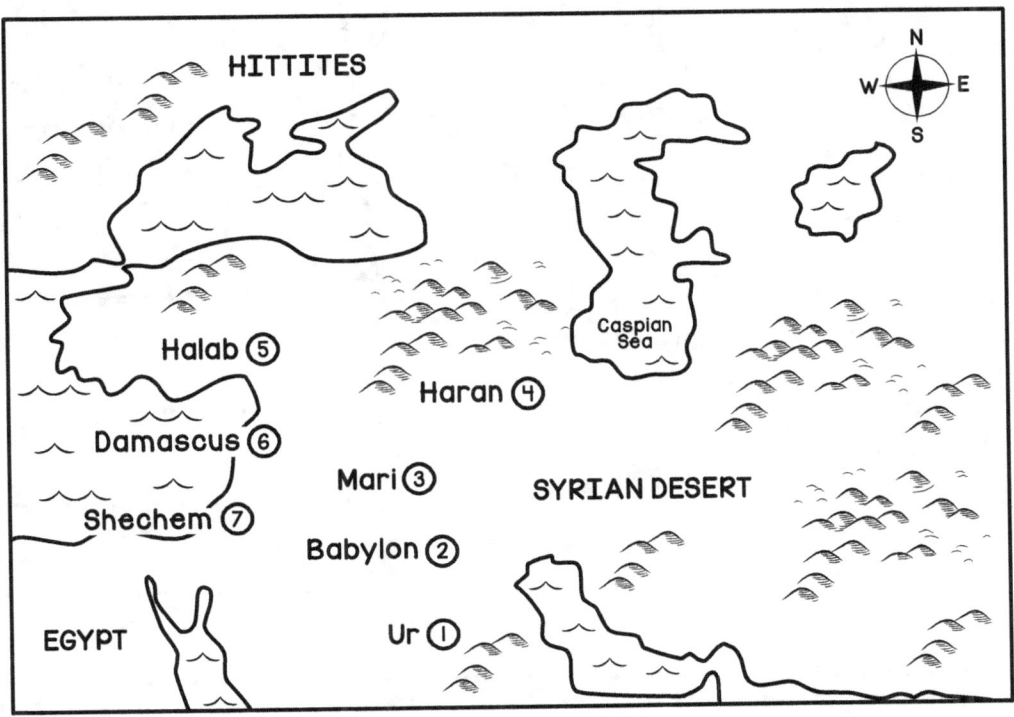

What items do you think Sarah took to Canaan with her? Research daily life in ancient Mesopotamia and make a list of items Sarai may have taken.

....

How did Abraham try to deceive Pharaoh?

....

How did God afflict Pharaoh?

....

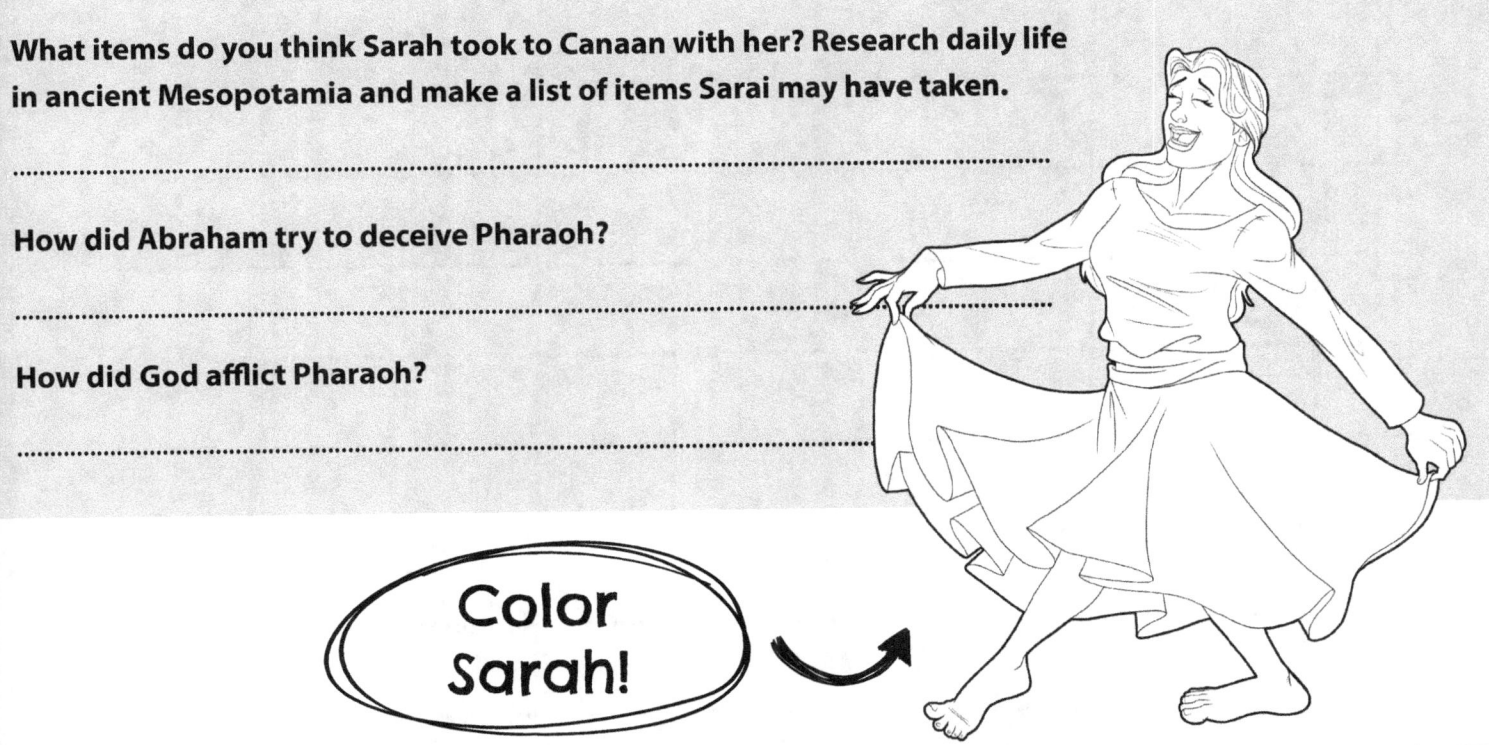

Color Sarah!

Let's Review

1. God used Sarah to...
2. What could Sarah's life teach me?
3. Summarize her story in 4-6 sentences.

....

....

....

....

....

....

....

....

....

....

....

REBEKAH

Read Genesis 24:1-67.
Answer the questions below.

1. Who was the father of Isaac? ....

2. Where did Abraham send his servant to find a wife for Isaac? ....

3. How many camels did the servant take with him? ....

4. Where did the servant find Rebekah? ....

5. What jewelry did the servant give Rebekah? ....

6. What was the name of Rebekah's father? ....

7. What did Rebekah do when she first saw Isaac? ....

8. How old was Isaac when he married Rebekah? ....

9. Where did Isaac and Rebekah live after they were married? ....

10. What were the names of Isaac and Rebekah's two sons? ....

Marriage in ancient Israel

The ancient Israelites viewed marriage differently to how we get married today. Marriage was about family, property and relationships. The exchanging of gifts, negotiations, bridal consent, wedding celebration and blessings were all part of the marriage process. Abraham's servant knew Rebekah was the answer to prayer. He gave her a gold ring and two gold bracelets for her arms (Genesis 24:1-28). In bestowing these pieces of jewelry, he claimed Rebekah for Isaac. In accepting these pieces of jewelry, she allowed the servant to touch her wrists and face showing that she was willing to proceed. Discuss: how is marriage in your country today different from marriage in ancient Israel?

Design and decorate your own gold bracelet.

Let's Review

1. God used Rebekah to...
2. What could Rebekah's life teach me?
3. Summarize her story
   in 4-6 sentences

....

....

....

....

....

....

....

....

....

....

....

HAGAR

Read Genesis 16:1-34.
Answer the questions below.

1. What nationality was Hagar? ....

2. What was Hagar's job? ....

3. What was the name of Hagar's mistress? ....

4. How did Hagar react when she discovered she was pregnant? ....

5. What instructions did the Angel of God give Hagar by the spring? ....

6. What name did the Angel tell Hagar to call her child? ....

7. Who was the father of Hagar's child? ....

8. What two things did Abraham give Hagar when she left the camp? ....

9. After Hagar and her child left the camp, where did they go? ....

10. From which place did the Angel of God call to Hagar in the wilderness? ....

Who was Hagar?

Read Genesis 16:1-16 and 21:1-21. Complete the worksheet below.

Nationality:

....

Worked for:

....

Hagar had a .... named ....:

Hagar is most famous for:

....

....

Five words that describe Hagar:

1. ....

2. ....

3. ....

4. ....

5. ....

Name two things God did for Hagar:

....

....

Let's Review

1. Abraham used Hagar to...
2. What did God promise Hagar?
3. Summarize her story in 4-6 sentences.

....

....

....

....

....

....

....

....

....

....

....

RACHEL

Read Genesis 29:1-35:29.
Answer the questions below.

1. Who was Rachel's older sister? ....

2. What were the names of Rachel's two sons? ....

3. Who was Rachel's father? ....

4. How many years did Jacob agree to work for Rachel? ....

5. Who did Laban trick Jacob into marrying? ....

6. Which two sons of Bilhah did Rachel raise? ....

7. Which son of Rachel was Jacob's favorite child? ....

8. What possessions did Rachel steal from her father's tent? ....

9. Where did Rachel hide the stolen possessions? ....

10. Where did Jacob bury Rachel? ....

Jacob's family

According to the Bible, Jacob had two wives; Leah and Rachel (who were sisters), and two concubines, Bilhah and Zilpah. Rachel and Leah did not object to the other women because it was their idea for Jacob to have more children with them (Genesis 30:3,9).

These four women had twelve sons between them. The sons of Leah were Reuben, Simeon, Levi, Judah, Issachar and Zebulun. The sons of Rachel were Joseph and Benjamin. The sons of Rachel's maidservant Bilhah were Dan and Naphtali, and the sons of Leah's maidservant Zilpah were Gad and Asher (Genesis 35:23-26). Jacob had at least one daughter, Dinah. There is little doubt that both Bilhah and Zilpah had a lower status than Leah and Rachel; the former were concubines, while Leah and Rachel were full-fledged wives. Their sons became the patriarchs of the 12 tribes of Israel.

1. How did Laban trick Jacob into first marrying Leah?

....

2. Who were the sons of Rachel?

....

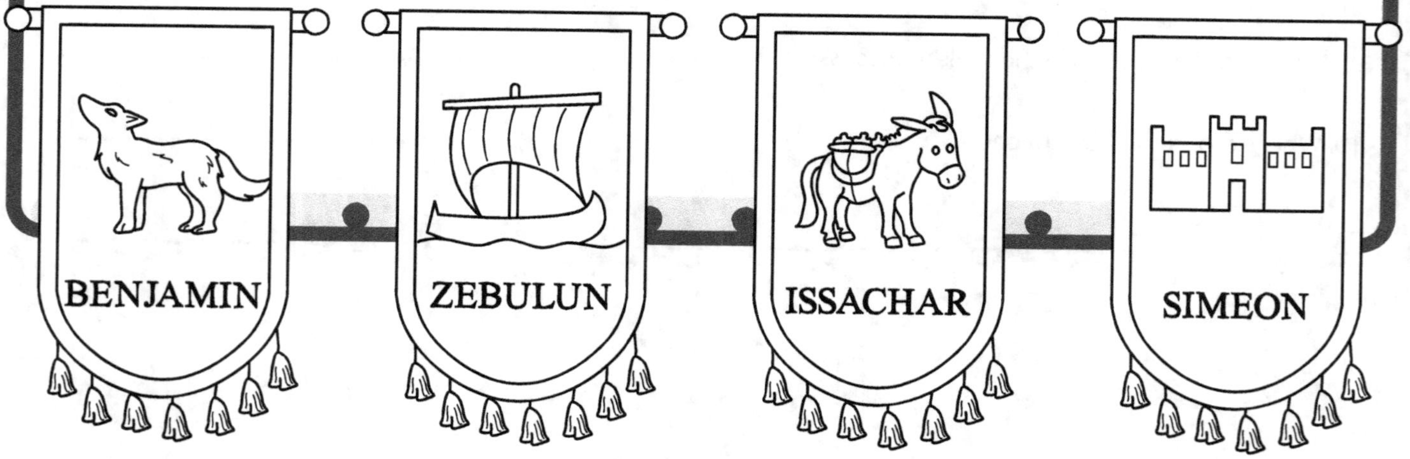

BENJAMIN   ZEBULUN   ISSACHAR   SIMEON

BENJAMIN

Let's Review

1. God used Rachel to...
2. What could Rachel's life teach me?
3. Summarize her story in 4-6 sentences.

....

....

....

....

....

....

....

....

....

....

....

MIRIAM

Read Exodus 2, 15 and Numbers 12.
Answer the questions below.

1. Who were Miriam's two brothers?

    ....

2. Who was Miriam's mother?

    ....

3. Why did Miriam wait in the reeds by the river?

    ....

4. Who did Miriam fetch to take care of the baby?

    ....

5. What did Miriam do after the Israelites crossed the Red Sea?

    ....

6. Why did Miriam speak against Moses? (Numbers 12)

    ....

7. How did God punish Miriam for speaking against Moses?

    ....

8. How long was Miriam put outside the camp?

    ....

9. Miriam was from which tribe of Israel?

    ....

10. In which land was Miriam born?

    ....

Baby MOSES

Read Exodus 1-2. Find and circle the words below.

```
V O M O S E S E R M J L Y S P
G O Q C W R R Y S F L O P N B
M I R I A M O O W A T P H D A
P G Q E M M O P G Y S I A A S
L A Y L S H Z A F W D T R O K
J A P U O H E B R E W C A R E
H V M Y N G W V S M U H O I T
V J Q T R J B L V F K Q H V M
D W X V B U M W W A T E R E V
O W W I G E S Z J W J Z S R M
I I I J U M C U V W S V E B Y
G K P L J C P A T T G Q P A D
R G Z B D Y D R E E D S C N C
V M O R N C H F G J R W E K C
E G Y P T N R M O T H E R C A
```

MIRIAM

HEBREW

REEDS

EGYPT

PAPYRUS

RIVERBANK

PHARAOH

BASKET

PITCH

MOTHER

MOSES

WATER

Let's Review

1. Miriam helped baby Moses by...
2. What could Miriam's life teach me?
3. Summarize her story in 4-6 sentences.

....

....

....

....

....

....

....

....

....

....

....

....

ZIPPORAH

Read Exodus 2:1-4:31 and 18:1-27.
Answer the questions below.

1. Who was Zipporah's father?

....

2. In which land did Miriam grow up?

....

3. How many sisters did Zipporah have?

....

4. Where did Zipporah meet her future husband?

....

5. What were the names of Zipporah's two sons?

....

6. On what type of animal did Zipporah and her sons leave Midian?

....

7. What did Zipporah do to her son on the journey to Egypt?

....

8. Why did Zipporah describe Moses as a 'bridegroom of blood'?

....

9. What is the meaning of the name 'Gershom'?

....

10. When Moses returned to Midian with the Israelites, where did

he meet Zipporah?

....

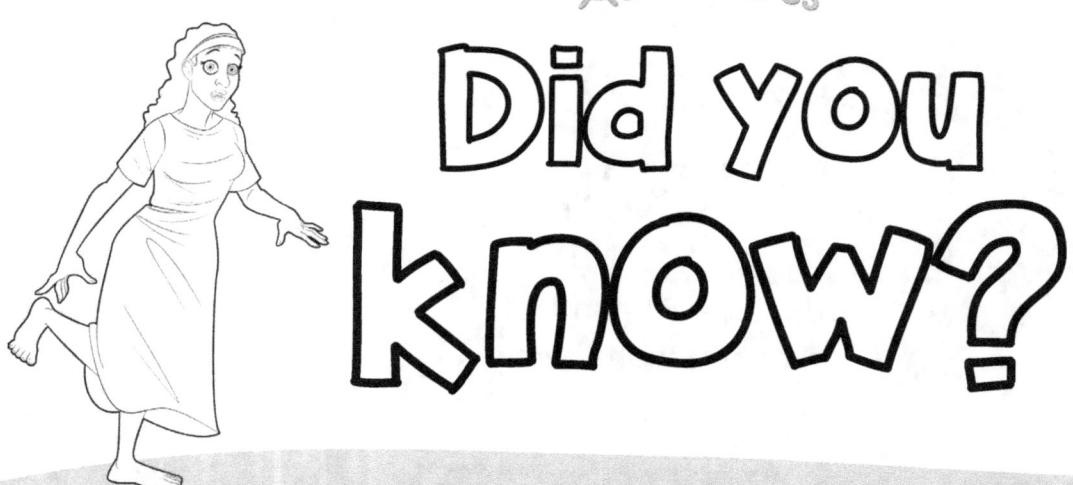

Did you know?

Zipporah was the wife of Moses and the daughter of Jethro, a priest of Midian. When Moses fled to the land of Midian, he met Zipporah and her six sisters. They were having trouble getting water for their flocks. Moses helped the women by driving the shepherds away. Zipporah and her sisters brought Moses back to their tent to meet their father. Moses later married Zipporah and began a new life as a shepherd in the land of Midian.

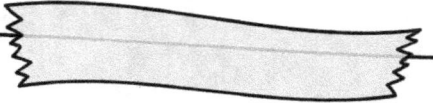

Moses and Zipporah had two sons; Gershom and Eliezer.
Use this space to draw Moses' family tree.

Let's Review

1. Zipporah helped Moses by...
2. Why do you think Moses sent Zipporah home? (Exodus 18)
3. Summarize her story in 4-6 sentences.

....

....

....

....

....

....

....

....

....

....

....

....

Bible Pathway Adventures

RAHAB

Read Joshua 2:1-24.
Answer the questions below.

1. Who sent the two spies to Jericho?

    ....

2. What place were the spies sent from?

    ....

3. Who were the two spies that went to Jericho?

    ....

4. Where in Jericho was Rahab's house?

    ....

5. How did Rahab hide the spies?

    ....

6. Who sent a message to Rabab telling her to bring out the spies?

    ....

7. Where did the king's men look for the spies?

    ....

8. How did Rahab help the spies escape?

    ....

9. Why did Joshua spare the lives of Rahab and her family?

    ....

10. How did Rahab mark her house so she was spared by the Israelites?

    ....

Canaanite Life

In Bible times, Canaanite and Israelite houses were very similar. Each house was made of mud-brick, had one to two floors with a courtyard, were flat-roofed, and were surrounded by a wall or fence. At night, animals were kept in the front courtyard to keep them safe from wild animals and robbers. Inside, the house typically had two floors; the top floor was for leisure and sleeping, and the bottom floor for cooking and storage. Kitchens were usually small rooms where food was prepared and cooked over a small cooking fire. Next to this room was a storage room for cooking utensils and food. It was important to store extra food as weather in the Middle East was often unpredictable. It was common to have a poor harvest once every four years.

A ladder or flight of stairs led to the top floor. This was a leisure area where families slept, and entertained themselves and guests by playing music, dancing, and playing board games. Another ladder led onto the roof where families slept in summer to keep cool. Roofs were also used for drying organic material like flax. This is where Rahab hid the spies from the king of Jericho.

Color the
Canaanite house!

How was each floor used by families?

....

Why do you think roofs were used to dry organic material like flax?

....

Let's Review

1. Rahab helped the Israelites by...
2. The Israelites spared Rahab's life because...
3. Summarize her story in 4-6 sentences.

....

....

....

....

....

....

....

....

....

....

....

RUTH

Read Ruth 1:1-4:17.
Answer the questions below.

1. Where was Ruth born?   ....

2. What was the name of Ruth's sister-in-law?   ....

3. Who was Ruth's first husband?   ....

4. With whom did Ruth move to Bethlehem?   ....

5. Where did Ruth and Boaz first meet?   ....

6. What did Boaz offer Ruth to eat?   ....

7. On the threshing floor, where did Ruth sleep?   ....

8. What did Boaz give Ruth the next morning?   ....

9. Boaz was of which tribe of Israel? (1 Chronicles 2)   ....

10. What did Ruth and Boaz name their son?   ....

Where YOU GO, I WILL GO. Where you stay, I WILL STAY. Your people shall be my PEOPLE & YOUR GOD my GOD

Ruth

(RUTH 1:16)

Let's Review

1. Ruth showed loyalty to Naomi by...
2. What could Ruth's life teach me?
3. Summarize her story in 4-6 sentences.

....

....

....

....

....

....

....

....

....

....

....

NAOMI

Read Ruth 1-3.
Answer the questions below.

1. What were the names of Naomi's two daughters-in-law? ....

2. Who was Naomi's husband? ....

3. What were the names of Naomi's two sons? ....

4. In which land did Naomi's husband and sons die? ....

5. What nationality were Naomi's daughters-in-law? ....

6. Which daughter-in-law left Moab with Naomi? ....

7. To which Israelite town did Naomi and Ruth travel? ....

8. Naomi and Ruth arrived in the town at the start of which harvest? ....

9. What name did Naomi tell the people to call her? ....

10. Who did Ruth marry? ....

Who was Naomi?

Read Ruth 1:1-4:22. Complete the worksheet below.

Lived in:

....

Married to:

....

Daughters-in-law:

....

Naomi is most famous for:

....

....

Five words that describe Naomi:

1. ....

2. ....

3. ....

4. ....

5. ....

Three important facts about Naomi:

....

....

Let's Review

1. Naomi returned to Bethlehem because...
2. What could Naomi's life teach me?
3. Summarize her story in 4-6 sentences.

....

....

....

....

....

....

....

....

....

....

....

....

DEBORAH

Read Judges 4:1-24.
Answer the questions below.

1. Who was Deborah's husband?   ....

2. What were Deborah's two roles?   ....

3. Where did Deborah sit to give judgment?   ....

4. Who did Deborah tell to lead the Israelites in a battle against

   the Canaanites?   ....

5. Who was the king of Canaan?   ....

6. What did Barak tell Deborah?   ....

7. How many men went into battle against the Canaanites?   ....

8. In which place did Barak attack the Canaanites?   ....

9. In whose tent did Sisera hide?   ....

10. Which woman killed Sisera?   ....

God's battle instructions

Deborah was a prophet and judge of Israel. A true prophet says what God wants them to say. God gave Deborah battle instructions for Barak. Unscramble the words to learn God's instructions. *Hint: Read Judges 4:6-7 (ESV)*

erGtah 0l,000 nme rfmo hte sbetir

_____

fo hlNtaipa nda uuZnble. daeL hmte

_____

ot tnMou bTora. I llwi ekma eriaSs,

_____

eth merndomac fo gKin ibnaJ's

_____

myar, omce ot oyu.

_____

Let's Review

1. Deborah told Barak to...
2. What could Deborah's life teach me?
3. Summarize her story
in 4-6 sentences.

....

....

....

....

....

....

....

....

....

....

....

DELILAH

Read Judges 13:1-16:31.
Answer the questions below.

1. Who wanted to capture Samson?

....

2. For how many years did Samson judge the Israelites?

....

3. How much silver was Delilah offered to betray Samson?

....

4. What was Delilah's nationality?

....

5. Where did Delilah live?

....

6. What did Delilah use to first bind Samson?

....

7. What did Delilah use to bind Samson a second time?

....

8. How many locks of Samson's hair did Delilah weave into her loom?

....

9. What did Samson finally tell Delilah was the secret of his strength?

....

10. What happened after the Philistines captured Samson?

....

Match the scriptures

Learn the story of Samson and Delilah.
Match the Bible verse with the correct scripture.

"Trick Samson into telling you his secret. Then we will know how to capture him... If you do this, each one of us will give you 1,100 pieces of silver."

Judges 16:19

Samson went to sleep, Delilah used the loom to weave the seven braids of hair on his head.

Judges 16:14

"I have never had my hair cut. I was dedicated to God before I was born. If someone shaved my head, I would lose my strength. I would become as weak as any other man."

Judges 16:17

Delilah called in a man to shave off the seven braids of Samson's hair. In this way she made Samson weak, and his strength left him.

Judges 16:5

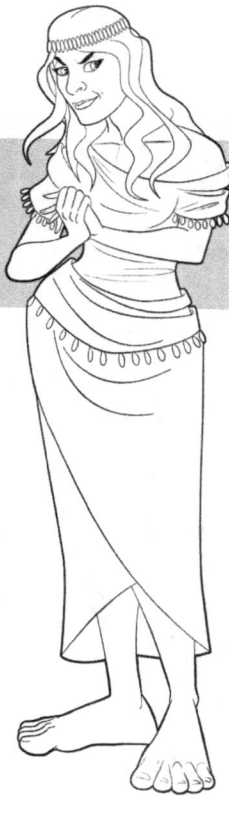

Let's Review

1. The Philistines used Delilah to...
2. How did Samson lose his strength?
3. Summarize her story in 4-6 sentences.

....

....

....

....

....

....

....

....

....

....

....

HANNAH

Read 1 Samuel 1:1-2:36.
Answer the questions below.

1. Who was Hannah's husband? ....

2. Why did Hannah's husband give her a double-portion? ....

3. Why did Peninnah provoke Hannah? ....

4. Why did Hannah cry bitterly at the temple? ....

5. What did Hannah promise God if He gave her a child? ....

6. What did Eli the priest think when he saw Hannah in the temple? ....

7. What name did Hannah give her son? ....

8. What did Hannah bring her son each year? ....

9. How many children did Hannah have after her first son? ....

10. Where was the temple located? ....

Nazarite rules

Hannah asked God for a son. In return, she vowed to give the son back to God for His service. She promised her son would stay a Nazarite all the days of his life. Nazarites follow special rules (Numbers 6:1-21). Match the rule with the picture.

Do not cut your hair ✂

Do not drink wine ✂

Do not eat grapes ✂

Do not eat unclean food ✂

Do not touch dead things ✂

Let's Review

1. God used Hannah to...
2. What could Hannah's life teach me?
3. Summarize her story
   in 4-6 sentences.

....

....

....

....

....

....

....

....

....

....

....

....

ABIGAIL

Read 1 Samuel 25 and 2 Samuel 3.
Answer the questions below.

1. What two characteristics describe Abigail? ....

2. In which place did Abigail live with her husband? ....

3. Who was Abigail's first husband? ....

4. How did Nabal react to David's request for provisions? ....

5. How did Abigail prevent David from killing Nabal? ....

6. How did David react to Abigail's gifts? ....

7. Why did Abigail not tell Nabal about her meeting with David when she first returned home? ....

8. What happened when Abigail finally told Nabal about the meeting? ....

9. After Nabal died, why did David send messengers to Abigail? ....

10. What was the name of Abigail's son? ....

Book of 1 Samuel

The
Israelite Times

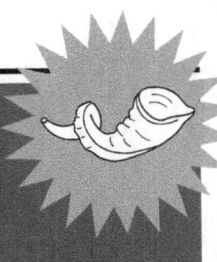

1 Samuel 25   WILDERNESS OF PARAN   A BIBLE HISTORY PUBLICATION

Abigail intervenes!

....

....

....

....

....

....

Nabal dies

David marries Abigail

....

....

....

....

Let's Review

1. Abigail helped David by...
2. What could Abigail's life teach me?
3. Summarize her story in 4-6 sentences.

....

....

....

....

....

....

....

....

....

....

....

BATHSHEBA

Read Matthew 1:6 and 2 Samuel 5, 10-12.
Answer the questions below.

1. Who was Bathsheba's father?   ....

2. In which city did David have a palace?   ....

3. Which two kingdoms did David rule?   ....

4. What was Bathsheba doing when David first saw her?   ....

5. Who did David arranged to be killed in battle?   ....

6. What did Bathsheba do when she heard Uriah had died? ....

7. In 2 Samuel 11, what message did Bathsheba send David? ....

8. Who confronted David about his adultery?   ....

9. Who became the king of Israel after David?   ....

10. Who was David's father?   ....

David and Bathsheba

Read 2 Samuel 11 and Exodus 20. Answer the questions below.

What did David do wrong?
(2 Samuel 11)

How did David deal with Uriah?

Why is the seventh commandment important?
(Exodus 20:14)

How did Nathan rebuke David?

What happened to David and Bathsheba's child?

Let's Review

1. After Uriah was gone, David...
2. What can the story of David &
Bathsheba teach me?
3. Summarize her story
in 4-6 sentences.

....

....

....

....

....

....

....

....

....

....

....

JEZEBEL

Read 1 Kings 16:1-21:29.
Answer the questions below.

1. Where did Elijah challenge the false prophets of Baal? ....

2. What were the names of Jezebel's three sons? ....

3. Who was Jezebel's husband? ....

4. What did Jezebel do to Naboth? ....

5. What did Ahab do when Elijah visited him? ....

6. Why did Elijah go to Beersheba? ....

7. Who was Jezebel's father? ....

8. Who did Jezebel encourage her husband to worship? ....

9. How did Ahab die? ....

10. How did Jezebel die? ....

Write a letter!

Read 1 Kings 21:1-12 (ESV). Imagine you are Jezebel.
In your own words, write a letter to the city elders about Naboth.
Include all the words below in your letter.

_____

_____

_____

_____

_____

_____

_____

_____

| FAST | PEOPLE | KING | CURSED |
| NABOTH | DEATH | STONE | CHARGE |

Let's Review

1. Jezebel deceived Ahab by...
2. What could Jezebel's life teach me?
3. Summarize her story in 4-6 sentences.

....

....

....

....

....

....

....

....

....

....

....

QUEEN OF SHEBA

Read 1 Kings 10:1-29.
Answer the questions below.

1. Why did the queen of Sheba visit Solomon? ....

2. What gifts did the queen bring with her? ....

3. How did the queen describe Solomon's servants? ....

4. What impressed the queen about Solomon? ....

5. What did the queen of Sheba say about Yahweh? ....

6. In which city was the temple? ....

7. Who was Solomon's mother? ....

8. What did Solomon do with the wood that Hiram brought him? ....

9. What gifts did Solomon give the queen? ....

10. After the queen and her servants left Jerusalem, where did they go? ....

I'm an Explorer!

Read 1 Kings 10:1-13. Imagine you are an explorer in the ancient Middle East. Practice your map making skills by adding directions to this map so the queen of Sheba can find her way to Jerusalem. Remember to include rivers, cities, mountains, and deserts.

MEDITERRANEAN SEA

Jerusalem

EGYPT

YEMEN

N
W   E
S

Let's Review

1. The queen traveled to Jerusalem to...
2. How did Solomon impress the queen?
3. Summarize her story in 4-6 sentences.

....

....

....

....

....

....

....

....

....

....

....

QUEEN VASHTI

Read Esther 1:1-2:18.
Answer the questions below.

1. Who was Vashti's husband?

....

2. Vashti was queen of which empire?

....

3. In which year of his reign did the king hold a huge banquet?

....

4. Where did Vashti hold a feast for the women?

....

5. Why did the king want to show Vashti to the people?

....

6. What did the king ask her to wear?

....

7. How did Vashti react to the king's request?

....

8. Who did the king ask for advice?

....

9. What punishment did Vashti receive for disobeying the king?

....

10. Who replaced Vashti as Queen of Persia?

....

Susa's royal complex

Queen Vashti lived at the royal palace in the city of Susa (Shushan), where she gave a feast for the women (Esther 1). Susa was an ancient city in Iran that became part of the Persian empire under Cyrus II, the Great. During the Achaemenian period, Susa was the winter capital of many Achaemenian kings. One of these kings, Darius the Great, built an impressive palace complex that included an audience hall, a monumental gate, and a royal residence, located on an artificially raised platform 15 meters (49 ft) high, covering 100 hectares (250 acres). It was entered from the east, where guests were welcomed at the Great Gate. Moving to the west, guests passed along three or four courts. The Third Court was larger than two first courts, and may have been used for military exercises.

The palace complex was destroyed by a fire during the reign of Artaxerxes I, and then restored fifty years later by his grandson. Alexander of Macedonia captured Susa in 330 BC, and seized 40,000 talents of gold and silver from the treasury. According to historians, in 324 BC, a huge marriage ceremony was held in the city of Susa. It included 10,000 men from the army of Alexander the Great!

1. List three facts about the royal palace.

   ....

2. Imagine you are Queen Vashti. What type of food would you serve at a feast for the women?

   ....

Color the royal palace!

Let's Review

1. Vashti refused to see her husband because...
2. I believe Vashti's punishment was...
3. Summarize her story in 4-6 sentences.

....

....

....

....

....

....

....

....

....

....

....

....

ESTHER

Read Esther 1:1-6:14.
Answer the questions below.

1. Who was the king of Persia? ....

2. Which family member did Mordecai help raise? ....

3. Who disobeyed the king by not coming when he commanded? ....

4. Why did Haman have a set of gallows made? ....

5. What instructions did Mordecai give Esther when she entered
   the palace? ....

6. What did Esther ask Mordecai and the Hebrews to do before
   she saw the king? ....

7. What did the king do when Esther came before him uninvited? ....

8. Who did Queen Esther invite to her banquets? ....

9. Who wanted to destroy all the Hebrews in the kingdom? ....

10. How did the king stop the destruction of the Hebrews? ....

Esther saved her people from destruction.
Unscramble the names to learn about
the people mentioned in this story.

ethEsr ....   stiVah ....

reMdcoai ....   serZeh ....

aHnma ....   hHaacht ....

ngiK Asushuaer ....   Tsrehe ....

✳ Read the story of Esther in Esther 1-10 (ESV).

Let's Review

1. God used Esther to...
2. What could Esther's life teach me?
3. Summarize her story
in 4-6 sentences.

....

....

....

....

....

....

....

....

....

....

....

ELIZABETH

Read Luke 1.
Answer the questions below.

1. Who was Elizabeth's husband?

....

2. Why did Elizabeth have no children?

....

3. Elizabeth was of which tribe of Israel?

....

4. Where did an angel appear to Elizabeth's husband?

....

5. What was the name of the angel?

....

6. What message did the angel give Elizabeth's husband?

....

7. What relation was Elizabeth to Mary, mother of Yeshua?

....

8. What did the baby do when Elizabeth heard Mary's greeting?

....

9. How long did Mary stay with Elizabeth?

....

10. How does the Bible describe Elizabeth?

....

The priesthood

Zechariah was the husband of Elizabeth, the father of John the Baptist, and a priest at the temple in Jerusalem. All priests were of the tribe of Levi, one of the 12 tribes of Israel. At the time of Yeshua (Jesus), there were approximately 7,000 priests in the land of Israel, divided into 24 clans. Each clan served at the temple twice a year. Most priests lived in country towns and villages but customarily went to Jerusalem to serve in the temple for a week each time. Their roles included offering sacrifices, taking care of the temple, priestly blessings, and teaching the Torah. Read Exodus 28, Leviticus 10-16, 21, Numbers 3, 6, 18-19, and Deuteronomy 17, 21, 33. Write six priestly roles in the boxes below.

www.biblepathwayadventures.com
Women of the Bible Activity Book

© BPA Publishing Ltd 2021

Let's Review

1. God used Elizabeth to...
2. What does the story of Elizabeth's pregnancy teach me?
3. Summarize her story in 4-6 sentences.

....

....

....

....

....

....

....

....

....

....

....

MARY

Read Matthew 1-2 and Luke 1-2.
Answer the questions below.

1. What was the relationship of Mary to Elizabeth?   ....

2. Who was the angel that appeared to Mary?   ....

3. What name did the angel tell Mary to call her son?   ....

4. Joseph was of which tribe of Israel?   ....

5. In which town did Mary live?   ....

6. Why did Mary and Joseph travel to Bethlehem?   ....

7. Which group of men visited Mary after Yeshua (Jesus) was born?   ....

8. How many Magi came to worship Yeshua?   ....

9. Which king wanted to destroy all the babies in Bethlehem?   ....

10. For which Appointed Time (Feast) did Mary and Joseph go to

    Jerusalem each year?   ....

An angel visits MARY

Read Luke 1 (ESV). Find and circle the words below.

```
B C N I P G Z R Y Q Y L N O K
B N H L A S N N E A E K N N N
Y H N I T N O S M N S Y M H J
K W O V L N G N Z B H Z T C Q
N C T L G D F E C J U Z Y Q N
A L L Z Y F M G L O A T G J A
O E I R X S X M N S L Q A M Z
V I R G I N P D K E N Z U O A
S L E U Q Y L I N P Y W E U R
C B F Z R H I F R H C C H S E
F H J U X C U O S I J A A M T
Y L L H Y Q T C M H T P X A H
O G R O P J A C O B Y J O R I
D M D V Q S E R V A N T K Y J
G G A L I L E E F C Y M Q I B
```

SON

VIRGIN

JACOB

HOLY SPIRIT

CHILD

NAZARETH

JOSEPH

GALILEE

MARY

SERVANT

ANGEL

YESHUA

Let's Review

1. God chose Mary to...
2. What could Mary's life teach me?
3. Summarize her story in 4-6 sentences.

....

....

....

....

....

....

....

....

....

....

....

....

ANNA THE PROPHETESS

Read Luke 2:1-40.
Answer the questions below.

1. In which town was Yeshua born?

    ....

2. In which city was the temple?

    ....

3. What had happened to Anna's husband?

    ....

4. Who was Anna's father?

    ....

5. What did Anna do at the temple every day?

    ....

6. How old was Anna when she saw Yeshua?

    ....

7. What happened when Anna saw Yeshua?

    ....

8. Anna was of which tribe of Israel?

    ....

9. What offering did Mary and Joseph make in the temple?

    ....

10. Who was king of Judea at this time?

    ....

Temple in Jerusalem

The temple in Jerusalem was the center of Hebrew life during biblical times. It began with the construction of the first temple by King Solomon, and ended with its destruction by the Romans in 70 AD. To house the ark of the covenant, King Solomon built the first temple in the tenth century, which was later destroyed by the Babylonians. They stole all its precious items and burnt what remained. A second temple was constructed during the time of Nehemiah and underwent major renovation during the reign of King Herod.

One of the reasons Herod enlarged the Temple Mount was to accommodate huge numbers of pilgrims coming to Jerusalem for the three pilgrimage Feasts: Passover and the Feast of Unleavened Bread, Shavu'ot, and Sukkot. It took 10,000 men ten years just to build the retaining walls! When they had finished, the platform was big enough to hold twenty-four football fields. People only had access to the temple courtyards and not the inside of the temple structure. But it was still considered a public building. It was also the meeting place of the Sanhedrin, the highest court of Jewish law during the time of Roman rule. When the time came for the purification rites required by the Torah, Joseph and Mary took Yeshua to the temple and presented him to God.

Color the temple!

Let's Review

1. God used Anna to...
2. What could Anna's faithfulness teach me?
3. Summarize her story in 4-6 sentences.

....

....

....

....

....

....

....

....

....

....

....

JAIRUS' DAUGHTER

Read Matthew 9:18-26 and Mark 5:21-43.
Answer the questions below.

1. Whose daughter had fallen asleep?   ....

2. Yeshua told the man, "Don't be afraid, just _____."   ....

3. Which three disciples went with Yeshua to the house?   ....

4. When Yeshua and His disciples arrived at Jairus' house,

   what was everyone doing?   ....

5. How old was Jairus' daughter?   ....

6. Why did the people at Jairus' house laugh at Yeshua?   ....

7. What did Yeshua say to Jairus' daughter while she was sleeping? ....

8. What happened after Jairus daughter woke up?   ....

9. In what region did this miracle take place?   ....

10. What instructions did Yeshua give Jairus and his family?   ....

Jairus' daughter

Read Mark 5:35-43 (ESV). Fill in the blanks below.

" While He was still speaking, there came from the ruler's house some who said, "Your daughter is dead. Why trouble the .... any further?" But overhearing what they said, Yeshua (Jesus) said to the ruler of the ...., "Do not fear, only ...." And He allowed no one to follow Him except ...., James, and John the brother of James. They came to the house of the .... of the synagogue, and Yeshua saw a commotion, people .... and wailing loudly. When He had entered, He said to them, "Why are you making a commotion and weeping? The .... is not dead but ...." And they laughed at Him. But He put them outside and took the child's .... and mother and those who were with Him and went in where the child was. Taking her by the hand, He said to her, "............................... cumi," which means, "Little girl, I say to you, ..." Immediately the .... got up and began walking (for she was 12 years of age), and they were immediately overcome with amazement. He strictly charged them that no one should know this, and told them to give her something to eat. "

SYNAGOGUE	TALITHA	FATHER
PETER	GIRL	ARISE
CHILD	TEACHER	BELIEVE
SLEEPING	WEEPING	RULER

Let's Review

1. A man named Jairus was...
2. Why was Yeshua not worried the girl had died?
3. Summarize this story in 4-6 sentences.

....

....

....

....

....

....

....

....

....

....

....

MARY & MARTHA

Read Matthew 26, Mark 14, Luke 10, and John 12.
Answer the questions below.

1. What relation was Mary to Martha?

....

2. What relation was Lazarus to Mary and Martha?

....

3. In which town did Mary and Martha live?

....

4. Who sat at Yeshua's feet to hear Him teach?

....

5. When Yeshua told the disciples Lazarus was sleeping,

what did He mean?

....

6. What did Yeshua do for Lazarus?

....

7. Who anointed Yeshua with perfume?

....

8. What type of perfume was used to anoint Yeshua?

....

9. Which disciple criticized the woman for wasting perfume?

....

10. Who was Martha's husband?

....

Are you Mary or Martha?

Yeshua (Jesus) entered a village, and a woman named Martha welcomed Him into her house. She had a sister called Mary, who sat at Yeshua's feet and listened to His teaching. But Martha was distracted with much serving. She went to Him and said, "Do you not care that my sister has left me to serve alone? Tell her to help me." But Yeshua answered, "Martha, Martha, you are anxious and troubled about many things, but one thing is necessary. Mary has chosen the good portion, which will not be taken away from her." *(Luke 10:38-42)*

Are you Mary or Martha? How do you put God first in your life?

....

....

....

....

....

....

Let's Review

1. Mary and Martha helped Yeshua by...
2. To choose 'the good portion' means...
3. Summarize their story in 4-6 sentences.

....

....

....

....

....

....

....

....

....

....

....

THE SAMARITAN WOMAN

Read John 4:1-45.
Answer the questions below.

1. At what time did Yeshua sit down near the well? ....

2. What was the name of the well where Yeshua talked with the woman? ....

3. Why did the woman come to the well? ....

4. From which region was the woman? ....

5. Why was the woman surprised that Yeshua asked her for a drink of water? ....

6. Where did Yeshua's disciples go while He spoke to the woman? ....

7. How many husbands had the woman had? ....

8. Who did Yeshua tell the woman was the Messiah? ....

9. Whoever _____ of the water I will give him will never be thirsty again. ....

10. Why did many Samaritans start to believe Yeshua was the Messiah? ....

Woman at the well

What do you think Yeshua meant when He said, "Everyone who drinks of this water will be thirsty again, but whoever drinks of the water that I give him will never be thirsty again. The water I give him will become in him a spring of water welling up to eternal life." (John 4:13-14) Write your answer in the space below. Color the picture.

Let's Review

1. Yeshua told the woman...
2. Who were the Samaritans?
3. Summarize her meeting with Yeshua in 4-6 sentences.

....

....

....

....

....

....

....

....

....

....

....

MARY MAGDALENE

Read Matthew 27-28, Luke 8, 24,
Mark 15-16, and John 19-20.
Answer the questions below.

1. How many demons did Yeshua cast out of Mary Magdalene? ....

2. Who stood at the foot of the cross with Mary Magdalene? ....

3. Who did Mary Magdalene see wrapping Yeshua's body in linen cloth? ....

4. After which weekly Appointed Time did Mary Magdalene,

   Mary and Salome buy burial spices? ....

5. What did they discuss on the way to the tomb? ....

6. Who told Mary Magdalene that Yeshua had risen? ....

7. Who did Yeshua first appear to after His resurrection? ....

8. When Yeshua spoke to Mary at the tomb, who did she think He was? ....

9. Why did Yeshua tell Mary Magdalene not to touch Him? ....

10. What did Mary Magdalene tell the disciples after she had seen Yeshua? ....

The empty tomb

Mary Magdalene went to the tomb where Yeshua (Jesus) was buried. He had risen!
What did she tell Peter? Color the picture and unscramble the words to find the answer.
Hint: Read John 20:2.

hTye ehav netak eth dLor uot fo eth bmto, nad ew

_____

od tno wonk rehew ythe evah ilad mhi.

_____

Let's Review

1. Mary Magdalene was a...
2. What could Mary's faithfulness teach me?
3. Summarize her story in 4-6 sentences.

....

....

....

....

....

....

....

....

....

....

....

....

PRISCILLA

Read Acts 18:1-4, 26:1-32, Romans 16:1-3,
1 Corinthians 16:1-19, and 2 Timothy.
Answer the questions below.

1. What was Priscilla's profession? ....

2. Who was Priscilla's husband? ....

3. Why did Priscilla leave Italy and go to Corinth? ....

4. In which city did Paul leave Priscilla and Aquila? ....

5. In Ephesus, which man did Priscilla and Aquila disciple? ....

6. In which city did Paul stay with Priscilla and Aquila? ....

7. In which place did Apollos teach the scriptures? ....

8. What were the only scriptures available at the time of Paul? ....

9. In 1 Corinthians 16:19, what happened on a regular

    basis in Priscilla's house? ....

10. In Romans 16:3, what did Priscilla and Aquila do for Paul? ....

Priscilla & Aquila's Profile

Aquila

Wife:...

Nationality: ....

Occupation: ....

Place of Birth: ....

Places visited: ....

Current address: ....

....

Priscilla

Husband: ....

Nationality: ....

Occupation: ....

Place of Birth: ....

Places visited: ....

Current address: ....

....

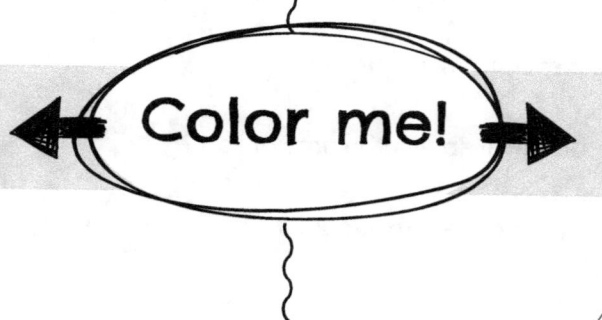

Color me!

Let's Review

1. Priscilla and Aquila traveled to...
2. What did Priscilla & Aquila have in common with Paul?
3. Summarize their story in 4-6 sentences.

....

....

....

....

....

....

....

....

....

....

....

LYDIA OF THYATIRA

Read Acts 16:1-40.
Answer the questions below.

1. In which city did Lydia live? ....

2. What was Lydia's profession? ....

3. In which city did Lydia meet Paul the apostle? ....

4. With whom was Paul traveling? ....

5. On which day of the week did Lydia meet Paul? ....

6. What happened after Lydia heard Paul speak about Yeshua? ....

7. Why was Paul thrown in prison? ....

8. Who did Paul visit after he was released from prison? ....

9. What type of colony was Philippi? ....

10. In which book of the Bible do we find the story of Lydia? ....

The purple cloth trade

Thyatira was the name of an ancient Greek city in Asia Minor, now the modern Turkish city of Akhisar. At the time of Paul, it was famous for its dyeing facilities and was a center of the purple cloth trade. Archaeologists have found inscriptions relating to the guild of dyers among the ancient ruins of the city.

Paul met Lydia in Philippi with other women along the riverbank. Lydia was originally from Thyatira, a busy merchant city of guilds. It is likely that Lydia learned her trade there. Although purple dye can be made from the madder plant, the only true purple colorfast dye at that time was made by the murex snail. Making purple dye was expensive and took a long time. A snail's gland secreted one drop of liquid, so it usually took about 10,000 shells to make a small amount of dye. No wonder purple dye was costly! As a result, purple dye was only purchased by royalty and wealthy people who used it to stripe a border of their garments. Lydia's clients would have likely been among the richest people in the city.

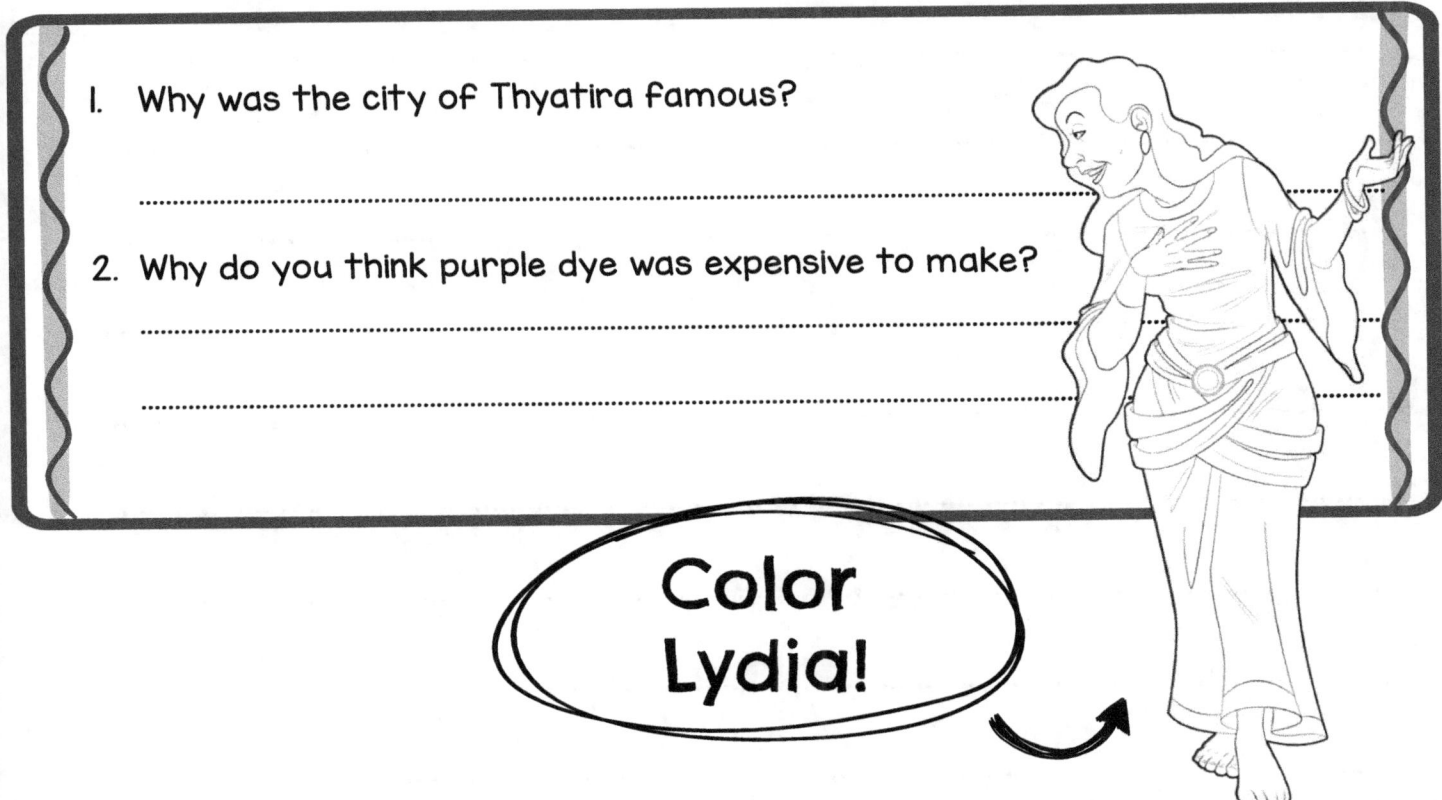

1. Why was the city of Thyatira famous?

....

2. Why do you think purple dye was expensive to make?

....

....

Color Lydia!

Let's Review

1. Lydia helped Paul by...
2. Lydia worshipped...
3. Summarize her story in 4-6 sentences.

....

....

....

....

....

....

....

....

....

....

....

....

TABITHA

Read Acts 9:32-43.
Answer the questions below.

1. Tabitha lived in which city? ....

2. Tabitha was a disciple of which famous teacher? ....

3. What is another name for Tabitha? ....

4. In Acts 9:36, how does the Bible describe Tabitha? ....

5. Why had Tabitha died? ....

6. How many men went to fetch Peter? ....

7. When Peter arrived, what were the widows doing? ....

8. What did Peter say to Tabitha? ....

9. What happened after Peter spoke to Tabitha? ....

10. Where did Peter stay while he visited Joppa? ....

Tabitha restored to life

Are the statements below TRUE or FALSE?
Read Acts 9:32-43. Circle the correct box below.

Tabitha was full of pride

Tabitha fell ill and died

Tabitha lived in Caesarea

The men took Peter to the upper room

Peter told Tabitha to cook a meal

Peter stayed in Joppa for many days with Simon

TRUE	FALSE
TRUE	FALSE
TRUE	FALSE
TRUE	FALSE
TRUE	FALSE
TRUE	FALSE

Why did many people start to believe in the Messiah?

Let's Review

1. God used Peter to...
2. Peter raised Tabitha to life because...
3. Summarize her story in 4-6 sentences.

....

....

....

....

....

....

....

....

....

....

SALOME

Read Matthew 14:1-12 and Mark 6:14-29.
Answer the questions below.

1. Who was Salome's father? ....

2. Who was Salome's mother? ....

3. Who attended Herod's banquet? ....

4. Why did Salome dance for Herod? ....

5. What did Herod say to Salome she could request? ....

6. What did Salome request from Herod? ....

7. What relation was Yeshua to John the Baptist? ....

8. Why had Herod imprisoned John the Baptist? ....

9. Where was John the Baptist beheaded? ....

10. What did the disciples do with John the Baptist's body? ....

Did you know?

Herod Antipas was a son of Herod the Great, who became king of Judea. He had John the Baptist thrown in prison for the sake of Herodias, his brother Philip's wife, because John had told him, "It's not lawful for you to have her." At Herod's birthday, the daughter of Herodias (Salome) danced before the guests and pleased him. He promised to give her whatever she wanted. Salome asked for John's head on a platter. Herod didn't want to break his promise to Salome. He had John executed, and his head brought on a platter and given to Salome.

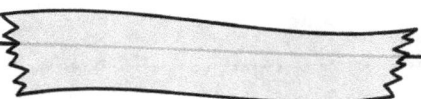

Read Matthew 14:1-12. Draw a scene from this Bible passage.

Let's Review

1. Salome was at Herod's party because...
2. How did Salome help kill John the Baptist?
3. Summarize her story in 4-6 sentences

ANSWER KEY

Bible quiz: Eve
1. Adam's rib
2. Garden of Eden
3. She was mother of all the living
4. A serpent
5. Tree of the knowledge of Good and Evil
6. He increased her pain during childbirth
7. The serpent tricked me
8. Made clothing out of fig leaves to cover themselves
9. Out of the garden
10. Cain, Abel, Seth, Awan, Azura, and Aclima

Bible word scramble: Eve
Adam, Eden, Eve, serpent, Abel, woman, man, Cain

Bible quiz: Sarah
1. Land of Canaan
2. Mesopotamia
3. Sarai
4. To escape the famine
5. Sarah was living in Pharaoh's house
6. 90 years' old
7. Isaac
8. Hagar
9. Wood
10. In the cave of the field of Machpelah before Mamre (Hebron)

Bible quiz: Rebekah
1. Abraham
2. Mesopotamia
3. Ten camels
4. By a spring
5. A gold ring and two bracelets
6. Bethuel
7. Covered herself with a veil
8. 40 years
9. The Negeb
10. Jacob and Esau

Bible quiz: Hagar
1. Egyptian
2. Servant / slave
3. Sarah
4. She looked at Sarah with contempt
5. Return to your mistress and submit to her
6. Ishmael

7. Abraham
8. Bread and water
9. Wilderness of Beersheba
10. From Heaven

Bible quiz: Rachel
1. Leah
2. Joseph and Benjamin
3. Laban
4. Seven years
5. Leah
6. Dan and Naphtali
7. Joseph
8. Household idols
9. In her camel's seat cushion
10. On the road to Efrat (Bethlehem)

Worksheet: Jacob's family
1. Laban substituted his older daughter, Leah, for Rachel at the wedding ceremony
2. Joseph and Benjamin

Bible quiz: Miriam
1. Moses and Aaron
2. Yocheved
3. To see what would happen to baby Moses
4. Miriam and Moses' mother
5. Took a tambourine in her hand and sang songs of praise
6. Because of the Cushite woman
7. Miriam became leprous
8. Seven days
9. Levi
10. Land of Egypt

Bible word search puzzle: Baby Moses

Bible quiz: Zipporah
1. Jethro
2. Land of Midian
3. Six sisters
4. By a well in the land of Midian
5. Gershom and Eliezer
6. A donkey
7. Took a flint and cut off his foreskin
8. Because of the circumcision
9. Sojourner in a foreign land
10. At Mount Sinai

Bible quiz: Rahab
1. Joshua
2. Shittim
3. The Bible does not say
4. In the city wall
5. Rahab hid the spied under flax on the roof of her house
6. King of Jericho
7. Jordan River
8. Used a rope to help the men escape through a window
9. Because Rahab hid the spies
10. Scarlet thread

Worksheet: Canaanite life
1. Bottom floors were used for cooking, storage, and the animals; top floors were used for sleeping and entertaining
2. Roofs offered space to spread out organic material, airflow, and heat from the sun

Bible quiz: Ruth
1. Land of Moab
2. Orpah
3. Mahlon
4. Naomi
5. Boaz's field
6. Bread and roasted grain
7. At Boaz's feet
8. Six measures of barley
9. Judah
10. Obed

Bible quiz: Naomi
1. Ruth and Orpah
2. Elimelech
3. Mahlon and Chilion
4. Land of Moab
5. Moabites
6. Ruth
7. Bethlehem
8. Barley harvest
9. Mara
10. Boaz

Bible quiz: Deborah
1. Lappidoth
2. Prophetess and judge
3. Under a palm tree between Ramah and Bethel
4. Barak
5. Jabin
6. "If you go with me, I will go."
7. Ten thousand (from the tribes of Naphtali and Zebulon)
8. Taanach
9. Heber
10. Jael, wife of Heber

Bible word unscramble: God's battle instructions
Gather 10,000 men from the tribes of Naphtali and Zebulun. Lead them to Mount Tabor. I will make Sisera, the commander of King Jabin's army, come to you.

Bible quiz: Delilah
1. The Philistines
2. Twenty years
3. 1,100 pieces of silver from each Philistine chief
4. Philistine
5. Valley of Sorek
6. Seven fresh bowstrings
7. New ropes
8. Seven locks His hair:
9. "If my head is shaved, then my strength will leave me…" (Judges 16)
10. They blinded Samson and put him in prison

Worksheet: Match the scriptures
1. Judges 16:5: "Trick Samson into telling you his secret. Then we will know how to capture him… If you do this, each one of us will give you 28 pounds of silver."
2. Judges 16:14: Samson went to sleep, Delilah used the loom to weave the seven braids of hair on his head.
3. Judges 16:17: "I have never had my hair cut. I was dedicated to God before I was born. If someone shaved my head, I would lose my strength. I would become as weak as any other man."
4. Judges 16:19: Delilah called in a man to shave off the seven braids of Samson's hair. In this way she made Samson weak, and his strength left him.

Bible quiz: Hannah
1. Elkanah
2. Because he loved her
3. Peninnah was able to bear children and Hannah had none
4. Because she could not have children
5. Her child would be set apart to serve God
6. Hannah was drunk
7. Samuel
8. A robe
9. Five children
10. Shiloh

Bible quiz: Abigail
1. Smart and beautiful
2. Carmel
3. Nabal
4. Nabal refused to give David provisions
5. Abigail took David gifts of food and wine, and spoke with him
6. David told Abigail he would not harm Nabal
7. Nabal was drunk
8. Nabal had a heart attack and died ten days later
9. To ask for Abigail's hand in marriage
10. Chileab (Daniel)

Bible quiz: Bathsheba
1. Eliam
2. Jerusalem
3. The kingdoms of Israel and Judah
4. Bathing
5. Uriah
6. She mourned his death
7. "I am pregnant."
8. Nathan the prophet
9. Solomon
10. Jesse

Bible quiz: Jezebel
1. Mount Carmel
2. Ahaziah, Jehoram, and Athaliah
3. Ahab
4. Jezebel had Naboth killed so Ahab could possess his vineyard
5. Put on sackcloth and ashes, and fasted
6. To flee from Jezebel
7. Ethbaal, King of Sidon
8. False gods like Baal and Asherah
9. In battle
10. Jezebel was thrown out of a window and trampled by horses

Bible quiz: Queen of Sheba
1. To test Solomon with difficult questions
2. Camels carrying spices, gold and precious stones
3. Happy
4. Solomon's palace, servants, food, his wisdom, and temple offerings
5. Blessed be Adonai, your God.
6. Jerusalem
7. Bathsheba
8. Make pillars for the temple and palace, and musical instruments
9. Everything the queen desired
10. The queen and her servants returned home

Bible quiz: Queen Vashti
1. King Ahasuerus
2. Persian empire
3. Third year of his reign
4. At the royal palace in Susa (Shushan)
5. Because she was beautiful
6. Her royal crown
7. Vashti refused to go and meet her husband
8. Wise Men (Magi)
9. Vashti was forbidden to appear before her husband again
10. Esther (Hadassah)

Worksheet: Susa's royal palace
The palace complex included an audience hall, a monumental gate, and a royal residence located on a raised platform 15 metres (49 ft) high, covering 100 hectares (250 acres), access to the palace complex was on a brick pavement from the south through the Royal City, the palace was entered from the east, where the visitors were welcomed at the Great Gate. Moving to the west, guests passed along three or four courts. The Third Court was larger than two first courts, and may have been used for military exercises

Bible quiz: Esther
1. King Ahasuerus (Xerxes)
2. Esther (Hadassah)
3. Queen Vashti
4. So that King Ahasuerus would hang Mordecai on them
5. "Do not tell anyone you are a Hebrew, or who I am."
6. Fast (not eat for a period of time)
7. Held out his golden scepter
8. The king & Haman
9. Haman
10. The king sent letters throughout Persia allowing the Hebrews to defend themselves

Bible word unscramble: Esther

Esther, Mordecai, Haman, King Ahasuerus, Vashti, Zeresh, Hathach, Teresh

Bible quiz: Elizabeth

1. Zechariah
2. Elizabeth was barren. This means she was unable to have children
3. Levi
4. At the temple
5. Gabriel
6. "You will have a son and you will name him John."
7. They were cousins
8. The baby leaped for joy in the womb
9. Three months
10. Elizabeth walked righteously before God and obeyed His commandments

Bible quiz: Mary

1. Mary and Elizabeth were relatives
2. Gabriel
3. Yeshua
4. Judah
5. Nazareth
6. To register for the census
7. Shepherds
8. The Bible doesn't say
9. King Herod
10. Feast of Unleavened Bread (including the Passover meal)

Bible word search puzzle: An angel visits Mary

Bible quiz: Anna the prophetess

1. Bethlehem
2. Jerusalem
3. He had died and she was a widow
4. Phanuel
5. Fasted and prayed
6. 84 years' old
7. She gave thanks to God
8. Asher
9. A pair of turtledoves, or two young pigeons
10. King Herod

Bible quiz: Jairus' daughter

1. A synagogue official named Jairus
2. believe (Mark 5:35)
3. Peter, James, and John
4. Weeping and wailing
5. Twelve years
6. Because Yeshua told them the girl was not dead but sleeping
7. "Little girl, get up!"
8. She got up and began walking
9. Galilee
10. To feed the girl, and not tell anyone what He had done

Worksheet: What's the Word?

While He was still speaking, there came from the ruler's house some who said, "Your daughter is dead. Why trouble the Teacher any further?" But overhearing what they said, Yeshua (Jesus) said to the ruler of the synagogue, "Do not fear, only believe." And He allowed no one to follow Him except Peter, James, and John the brother of James. They came to the house of the ruler of the synagogue, and Yeshua saw a commotion, people weeping and wailing loudly. When He had entered, He said to them, "Why are you making a commotion and weeping? The child is not dead but sleeping." And they laughed at Him. But He put them outside and took the child's father and mother and those who were with Him and went in where the child was. Taking her by the hand, He said to her, "Talitha cumi," which means, "Little girl, I say to you, arise." Immediately the girl got up and began walking (for she was 12 years of age), and they were immediately overcome with amazement. He strictly charged them that no one should know this, and told them to give her something to eat.

Bible quiz: Mary and Martha

1. Mary and Martha were sisters
2. Brother
3. In Bethany
4. Mary
5. Lazarus had died

5. Raised Lazarus from the dead
7. Mary
8. Spikenard
9. Judas
10. The Bible doesn't say

Bible quiz: The Samaritan woman
1. The sixth hour
2. Jacob's well
3. To draw water
4. Samaria
5. Because Jews had no dealings with Samaritans
6. Into Sychar to buy food
7. Five
8. Himself
9. drinks
10. Because of this woman's testimony

Bible quiz: Mary Magdalene
1. Seven demons
2. Yeshua's mother and her sister, and Mary wife of Clopas
3. Joseph of Arimathea
4. The Sabbath
5. Who will roll away the stone from the entrance of the tomb?
6. An Angel
7. Mary Magdalene
8. The gardener
9. He had not yet ascended to the Father
10. "I have seen Yeshua!"

Worksheet: The empty tomb
"They have taken the Lord out of the tomb, and we do not know where they have laid Him."

Bible quiz: Priscilla
1. Tent-maker
2. Aquila
3. Claudius ordered all Jews to leave Rome
4. Ephesus
5. Apollos
6. Corinth
7. In a synagogue
8. Old Testament
9. People gathered together
10. Risked their lives for him

Bible quiz: Lydia of Thyatira
1. Thyatira
2. Seller of purple dye
3. Philippi
4. Silas and Timothy
5. The Sabbath

6. She was baptized
7. He cast demons out of a slave girl who made her masters money
8. Lydia
9. A Roman colony
10. The book of Acts

Worksheet: The purple cloth trade
1. At the time of the apostle Paul, Thyatira was famous for its dyeing facilities
2. Making purple dye took a long time. A snail's gland secreted one drop of liquid, so it usually took about 10,000 shells to make a small amount of dye

Bible quiz: Tabitha (Dorcas)
1. Joppa
2. Yeshua
3. Dorcas
4. Full of good works and charity
5. She became ill
6. Two men
7. Weeping and showing people clothing that Tabitha had made
8. "Tabitha, arise."
9. She opened her eyes and sat up
10. Simon the tanner's house

Worksheet: Tabitha raised to life
Tabitha was full of pride: False
Tabitha fell ill and died: True
Tabitha lived in Caesarea: False
The men took Peter to the upper room: True
Peter told Tabitha to cook a meal: False
Peter stayed in Joppa for many days with Simon: True

Bible quiz: Salome
1. Herod II
2. Herodias
3. Nobles and military commanders and the leading men of Galilee
4. It was Herod's birthday
5. Anything Salome desired
6. The head of John the Baptist
7. Yeshua and John were cousins
8. John criticized Herod for marrying his brother's wife
9. In prison
10. The disciple laid John's body in a tomb

◆◇ DISCOVER MORE ACTIVITY BOOKS! ◇◆

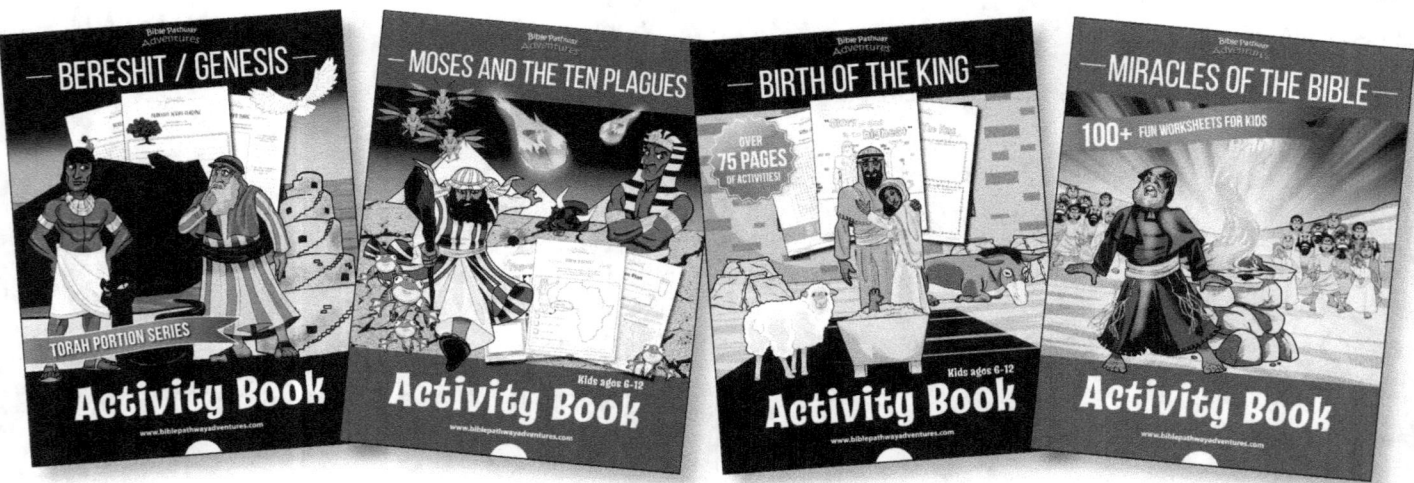

Available for purchase at www.biblepathwayadventures.com